Emotional Intelligence

An Organic Journey to The Center of Yourself

T.G. Benfield

Introduction

Some of us find it difficult to connect in the modern world, both with others and ourselves. An important factor that influences this connection is emotional intelligence, or "EQ" as it is often referred. When it comes to successes and happiness in our careers, relationships, and individual goals, emotional intelligence is of paramount importance. In fact, many professionals agree that EQ is just as important as IQ. However, this book is not about which one is more important. The following information seeks to shed some light on this very mysterious, internal and subjective topic.

Most will agree you need emotional intelligence to turn your intentions into actions, to make sound decisions regarding things that are of importance to you, and to connect with those around you in nurturing and productive ways. It is clear that emotional intelligence plays a significant role in our lives – both professional and personal. It has become the hallmark to determine the way a person works to achieve his or her organizational and personal goals.

Firstly I would like to congratulate you. Your decision to read this book tells me that you are determined to change your life for the better by enhancing your emotional intelligence. I will not sugarcoat the journey to the center of yourself, but what you should understand is that it won't necessarily be easy and some parts may be difficult, or even cause you mild emotional pain. However, at the end of the day you will realize that the journey is worth it and the issues I elaborate on here are more than worth confronting.

Upon reaching the last word of this book, you will realize that you have become an expert in the most imperative thing in the world – You! In fact, no one else can know you more than you know yourself. This book will change how you think of yourself and how you behave. These changes, though they may appear small, will result in significant changes in your life over time.

CONTENTS

CHAPTER 1: UNDERSTANDING EMOTIONAL INTELLIGENCE

What is emotional intelligence?

Emotional intelligence is the ability to identify, use, understand, and manage your emotions in positives ways to communicate effectively, overcome challenges, empathize with others, diffuse conflicts, and relieve stress. It is that 'intangible' something inside you that affects how you manage behavior, navigate social complexities, and make decisions to achieve the desired results.

It is important to note that emotional intelligence is different from how we perceive intellectual ability. Emotional ability is not acquired, it is learned. Learning emotional intelligence can take part at any point of one's life, and therefore, it is something you can have or develop within yourself. As a child you will be likely to absorb the emotional tendencies of your parents because you have surrounded yourself with them for so long. You may be underdeveloped in this area; perhaps this is why you have picked up this book? Or maybe you are just after an interesting read having not encountered this topic before. Either way, I will unearth this topic as best I can and provide practical advice in which you can apply to your own situations.

Remember that there is a variation between learning emotional intelligence and applying the knowledge to your life. Knowing that you should do something does not mean that you will do it, especially when you are overwhelmed by stress. Therefore, learning how to overcome stress appears to be the first step in becoming more emotionally aware.

Emotional intelligence is made up of various skills that fall under personal and social competence.

Your **personal competence** comprises of self-management and self-awareness, skills that focus on yourself rather than how you interact with people. Personal competence refers to your ability to understand your emotions, manage your behavior, as well as your tendencies.

On the other hand, **social competence** refers to your ability to comprehend other people's behavior, motives, and moods to enhance the quality of your relationships. From this definition, it is clear that relationship management skills and social awareness form the core of social competence.

Wait a moment. Have you realized that the journey to the center of yourself is now clear? All you need is to thoroughly understand your personal and social competence and learn how you can enhance the core of your emotional intelligence (self-management, self-awareness, social awareness, and relationships management skills). We will go into detail about this further down the track and suggest how you might go about unearthing these areas within yourself.

Principles of emotional intelligence

Since you now know what emotional intelligence is, let's explore the topic further for a better understanding of our inner selves. Caruso and Salovey (2004), in a report titled Emotional Intelligence: Theory, Findings, and Implications, revealed that emotional intelligence starts with the following principles.

1. Emotions are information

Emotions are reactions you have to different interactions and situations around you every day. Your emotional responses enable you to respond, adapt, and thrive in the environment you live. They can however be overwhelming at times and giving in to certain emotions can have poor outcomes for yourself and others around you. Therefore, your responses, whether negative or positive, could be perceived as 'data' or signals of how you think in different situations. With that, if you are mindful of what your emotions are signaling, you can consciously bring out a positive outcome whatever the situation.

2. Emotions cannot be ignored

Our judgments, emotions, and thinking are interconnected. The way we respond emotionally to situations, co-workers, and family has impacts on our job performance and relationships. Research done by Roy Baumeister, a social psychologist, which has been cited in Caruso and Salovey, revealed that individuals remember less information when they try to suppress their emotions.

Roy Baumeister explained that listening and information skills are negatively affected whenever someone tries to suppress their emotions. With that, you need to understand and reframe the real meaning of the information and emotional component without suppressing your emotions.

3. We can't hide emotions

Both unconscious and conscious attempts to mask your emotions will always fail. Research on facial expressions and lying by Ekman (cited in Caruso and Salovey 2004) proved that it is possible to tell if one is lying by observing his speech errors, pauses during his speech, and momentary emotional display.

'Surface acting' or covering emotions is associated with job burnout and other issues. Note that the desire to hide your emotions or engage in rational pursuits result in mistrust and pathetic decision-making.

4. Decisions should incorporate emotions for effectiveness

Effective management and interpersonal skills require the integration of associated emotions and pertinent information. Note that avoiding conflict or making everyone happy may not always end up in such successful decision-making.

We should appreciate the fact that the emotional intelligence theory recognizes that it is our emotions that make us humans. Therefore, we should embrace them and incorporate them into our daily lives.

5. Emotions follow logical patterns

Emotions are reactionary for different reasons and typically follow a particular pattern from low to high intensity depending on the thought or event that caused the emotion to arise. Therefore, emotions are not random.

6. Emotion universals and specifics

Emotional intelligence can be applied worldwide because rules governing emotions are universal. Though cultural differences, social behavior, and customs vary from one country to another, emotional expressions don't vary from one geographic location to another. Laughter, smiles, or tears for example are interpreted the same way globally.

Emotional intelligence, IQ, and personality

People have a tendency to perceive emotional intelligence as IQ, however, this is not correct. You need to understand that emotional intelligence taps an elementary aspect of human behavior that is different from one's intellect and is almost entirely subjective. Note that there is no connection between one's IQ and emotional intelligence.

IQ is consistent with ones ability to learn; furthermore, it's the same at the age of 17 as it is at age 53! On the contrary, emotional intelligence is a flexible set of skills that you can acquire and enhance at any time. Though some people appear to be more emotionally intelligent naturally, you can learn and enhance your emotional intelligence even if you were not born with it. If you continue reading further I will suggest some of the ways you can go about this.

Having now differentiated IQ and emotional intelligence, there is one thing that is ringing in your mind right now – personality. Personality is the stable 'style' that defines you. It is the outcome of your 'hard-wired' preferences including your inclination towards extroversion and introversion.

It is important to understand that just like one's IQ, personality cannot be used to determine one's emotional intelligence. However, it is mostly stable over one's lifetime, and you can neither learn it nor change it.

From the above discussion regarding IQ, EQ (emotional intelligence) and personality, it is evident that IQ and EQ are similar, but not the same. So, which one is more important? IQ or EQ?

At one point, IQ (a measure of your ability the think and reason) was perceived as the primary determinant of one's success. Those with high IQ levels/scores people would generally assume would have a life filled with success and accomplishment. This perception resulted in a heated debate whether IQ was a product of the environment or genes.

With time, it was realized that high IQ was not a guarantee of one's success in life. Also, IQ is such a narrow concept to fully encompass the broad range of one's knowledge and abilities. However, we cannot dismiss IQ because it is a significant element that contributes to success when it comes to scaling heights in certain areas, particularly academics.

People who have higher IQ perform well in school, perhaps get good jobs that have a decent income and tend be healthy. Do you attribute such success solely to one's IQ? Today, experts appreciate the fact that one's IQ is not the only determinant of one's success. Instead, it is a constituent of a complex array of influences that includes, among other things, emotional intelligence (EQ).

With that, the concept of emotional intelligence has a significant impact on various areas, particularly the business world. Note that currently most corporations mandate emotional intelligence education and are utilizing emotional intelligence tests as part of their selection and hiring processes.

Numerous research papers have revealed that people with great leadership skills tend to be more emotionally intelligent, and this implies that high emotional intelligence is a crucial quality that business managers and leaders should have. When managers can properly understand other employees on an emotional level it really opens up a whole world of connection and is a cornerstone for building rapport.

I would bet you have met someone who had low emotional intelligence: you are talking discreetly about a work problem you are having with a group of colleagues. John (low in emotional intelligence) doesn't recognize the present situation and inappropriately walks up enthusiastically to announce that he has won $100 lottery ticket and starts bragging!

Why is Emotional Intelligence Important?

In the recent past, the concept of emotional intelligence has become a hot topic especially on explaining how it affects today's workforce. Business is essentially a group of people, so anything that influences the effectiveness of a person's mind also affects the business one way or another.

As previously mentioned, many experts currently perceive a person's emotional intelligence to be of greater importance than the IQ. Furthermore, it can be used to predict one's level of success, overall happiness and quality of relationships. So, why is emotional intelligence so crucial for someone to grasp? The following paragraphs will subsequently answer this question for you.

Conflict resolution

Resolving conflicts or avoiding them before they start involves discerning other people's emotions and empathizing with their perspective. With that alone, you can be good at conflict resolution. Furthermore, you will become better at negotiation because of your ability to comprehend the desires and needs of other people.

Physical health

The ability to manage stress, which has negative impacts on your body and overall wellness, is strongly tied to your emotional intelligence. The only effective way of managing stress and maintain good health is by being aware of your emotional state and your reactions towards stress. Frequently people will consume caffeine and alcohol in their daily life. This is definitely something to stay away from or strictly limit if you find yourself stressed and anxious, for whatever reason. Physical activity and sleep are also critical in managing those stress levels, so make sure you get in the recommended quotas of each. Additionally, sharing your stress with someone you are open with, like your partner, boyfriend or girlfriend, will help to relieve the situation.

Relationships

Understanding and managing your emotions will enable you to communicate your feelings in a more constructive way. Also, you will be better placed to understand and relate to those you have relationships with e.g.: Family, friends, girl/boyfriend, workmates, you get the idea. Understanding the feelings, responses, and the needs of those you care about results in more fulfilling and stronger relationships.

Mental well-being

Emotional intelligence has a direct impact on our general outlook in life as well as our attitude. It can help in heightening your happiness; avoiding depression as well as mood swings. Furthermore, a heightened emotional intelligence correlates with a happier outlook on life and a positive attitude, something most of us strive for.

Leadership

In leadership, one of the most important qualities is the ability to relate in a positive manner, build strong relationships with other people, and understand what motivates others. This is the reason people with high emotional intelligence are usually better leaders. An effective leader should understand the needs of his/her people to device strategies to meet those needs in a way that encourages satisfaction at the workplace as well as performance. Emotionally savvy and intelligent leaders can strategically utilize the emotional diversity of the team members to build strong teams.

As you can see the emotions play a significant role in the overall quality of your professional and personal life, often being the driving force.

CHAPTER 2: EMOTIONS
What are emotions?

The term 'emotion' has different meanings. You need to know that there is a distinction between feelings and emotions, that feelings are the response part or function of the action. On the other hand, emotions include the experience or situation, interpretation and perception of the experience in the context of a specific situation.

Emotions have both physical and psychological aspects. They bridge your thoughts, feelings, and actions. This implies that emotions operate in every part of you, affecting every aspect of you, all encompassing. They indicate how things are going in your life. They keep you on the right track by ensuring the intellectual faculties of perception; memory, thought, and reason are not solely responsible for leading you in the most appropriate and logical direction.

Emotions control what you think, your actions, your overall behavior... It is clearly evident that people who dismiss, ignore, or repress their emotions are preparing their bodies for illness. This is because unreleased emotions can cause stress that in the worst cases can result in serious illnesses.

There is a common concept that can help us to understand emotions better – belief systems. Much of your underlying behavior is what is known as a belief system. This is a complex system based on a series of beliefs and is not necessarily confined to religion. It is within you, and filters all that you see and hear. It even influences how you behave in your daily life. There could be numerous elements that affect your daily life, just note that your belief system in this life has a significant effect on what you think and do.

It is important to understand that our belief systems affect our perceptions or how we interpret what we see, feel, and hear. Therefore, in your journey to the center of yourself, do the first things first. Deal with your belief system before you handle the identification process and release your emotions.

I am well aware that it takes a lot of work to analyze yourself and spot the beliefs that have a negative impact on your life. However, keep in mind that understanding your beliefs will give you a sound basis for emotional freedom. Therefore, the journey is worth it.

The core emotions

There are fundamentally two core emotions that anyone can experience – fear and love (opposites). All other emotions are various forms of these emotions. Note that behavior and thoughts come from either a place of fear or love. Emotions like depression, shame, sadness, anxiety, control, anger, confusion, inadequacy, hurt, guilt, and other similar emotions are fear-based emotions. On the other hand, emotions such happiness, trust, joy, contentment, caring, joy, and other similar emotions are love-based emotions.

Each of the above emotions can have varying degrees, with some being mild, moderate, or strong. For example, you can experience mild anger as dismay or disgust, at a moderate level, you can feel exasperated or offended, and at an intense level, you can feel hate or range. Note that the emotion that underpins anger is fear.

It is worth noting that we can't control our emotions. Instead, we can learn how to be with them, live peacefully with them, release them, and manage them, but it is hard to control them.

Think of a person who goes along day after day seeming to function normally, but suddenly he explodes in anger at something that is harmless. Anyone may wonder what would be wrong with that person, but the answer is simple – this is a sign of trying to control emotions, but they are leaking out!

The more you try to control your emotions, the more they will resist the control, and you may end up more frightened. Those around you may interpret this as 'loss of emotional control.'

Repressing emotions

When people encounter an experience that they find difficult or painful, they either get afraid or are unable to cope with the pain. Often they will dismiss the emotion and either exercise more, get busy, pretend nothing happened, drink more and eat more... All these activities are geared towards repressing rather than addressing the issue at hand.

We know emotions remain internally, in your stomach, muscles, and ligaments. They remain buried inside you until you bring them up and release them. Such emotions affect your relationships as well as your ability to grow spiritually and shift your level of consciousness. If you're not evolving to become the best version of yourself you are in fact de-evolving. You can't stay the same because that's unstable and not how the system works.

When we repress emotions, our behavior and reactions to present events are influenced by past events. This has a negative impact on relationships in your life. In fact, you can't be fully present with those whom you care for unless you shed off your emotions from the past events that are troubling you in some way.

You could have buried these emotions because they were painful, but your today's reactions are still affected by the repressed emotions. Therefore, for you to relate, understand, and respond to events in a sober way, you need to release your repressed emotion. Now, how you go about doing this is entirely up to you. You will know how to resolve the inner conflict if you're looking in the right places. Keep in mind that your real purpose is to maintain an increasing level of consciousness, lower entropy and live a love-based life.

Commit to emotional health

Individuals who make a deep commitment to becoming emotionally healthy are willing to scale the heights of their emotions and find emotional release. I will now help you to go through this journey of identifying your issues in an attempt to release some of those repressed emotions.

Identifying emotions

As said earlier in this chapter, emotions are indicators of what is going on in your life. With that, it is important to identify and release any buried emotion for you to improve how you relate to other people. Here are a few methods to help you in identifying your emotions.

Listen to your daydreams and thoughts

Sometimes we become so accustomed to thinking in particular patterns that we become unconscious about our daydreams and thoughts. To identify your emotions, hold your thoughts and catch your daydreams and then bring them to your present and conscious mind. This will reveal to you what you love or hate about your relationships or whatever it is you've been thinking about.

It is also wise to write down these thoughts and daydreams in your diary to understand and organize your thought patterns. If you maintain a written record of your thoughts for some time, you will be able to define your thinking patterns, and this presents a better chance for you to identify your emotions. Remember this sort of investigation is entirely subjective and it is your responsibility to be the detective and put the pieces of the puzzle together. This data you're ingesting at the present moment is supposed to give you support, suggestions and point you in the right direction.

Record things that make you feel strong

Maintain a record of what arouses strong emotions in you for several weeks. Note down what makes you have strong emotions, be it children, husband, weather, traffic jam, your fellow church members, whoever and whatever, add it to your list. Also, try to spot what makes you angry. One thing you should know about anger is that sadness is a mask covering anger and that anger is propelled by fear.

Therefore, for us to achieve emotional health, we need to identify what you are afraid of having or losing. Additionally this will help us to interpret our situations with greater clarity, enhance our awareness and help us take our emotional intelligence to a new level.

Get to know your 'small and insignificant hurts'

Most people ignore emotions and say that it doesn't matter, or it's not important yet; they have been hurt, and they are repressing these emotions. Keep in mind every small hurt that you continue to remember may combine with other repressed emotions and interfere with how you relate to other people. Instead of repressing, write these small hurts down and analyze each of them. This will help to identify your unexpressed emotions.

Be more specific about your emotions

Sometimes, you can get confused while trying to identify your emotions because you generalize everything. For example, you may be bored, experiencing loneliness, or stressed because you lack something. If you call this depression, it will be very difficult for you to release the emotion. Therefore, it is important to single out what you feel rather than generalizing it or self-diagnosing yourself with a mental disorder of sorts.

How to release emotions

For you to earn emotional freedom, you need to stop being afraid of your emotions. Don't even run away from them or fight them. Instead, accept them regardless of how they are. You were born with them, it is part of the human condition and they are neither bad nor good. You need to understand that **emotions dissipate and gradually disappear if you recognize them, feel them, and let them join your present**. Close your eyes and feel them as deeply as possible.

Set a good response to your emotions

After identifying a particular emotion, you need to decide how you will be responding to the emotion. Kindly note that there are numerous approaches you can take while responding to your emotions but some have serious effects. Therefore, it is advisable to analyze each approach carefully before acting. For example, the way you could respond to anger when you lose your marriage is different from how you will respond to anger when your kid drops your expensive iPad in boiling water.

Here are a few questions you should first answer when deciding how to respond to different events, bearing in mind that each situation and each emotion is different.

- Could I be partially responding to a past experience or it's purely what is happening now?

- Can I discuss the issue at hand now with the other person without paving a way for anger?

- Will I disclose my feelings to the other person?

- Is direct approach the suitable way to proceed?

- What would be the outcomes of directly dealing with the person or the situation?

- What do I anticipate from this discussion?

- Are my anticipations realistic or unrealistic?

- Should I approach someone else about the issue before doing anything?

Answering these questions honestly will help you to respond to your emotions well. For example, if your anger has reached a high level already, you may need to release it first before handling the situation you are facing.

Release your emotions physically

There are various ways of releasing emotions physically, especially emotions related to anger. Please ensure that you are not affecting anyone just because you are releasing your emotions. Otherwise, you will be creating more problems for yourself.

Go out for a drive, or into an empty room and scream. Scream as loud as you can and yell "I hate" as many times as you feel like if you are sure that this will drive away your anger. You can also cry until all your anger disappears. If this never works for you, please don't try as it may make your emotion worse.

If you are allergic to loud screams like me, just close your eyes and imagine that you are screaming away your hurt, pain, and rage. Imagine it, hear it, see it, and feel it as deeply as possible.

Some people tend to become physical when they are hurt. If you belong to this category, please don't release your emotions on anyone. Otherwise, you may get into further complications if you act in a violent manner; the law is likely to get involved. Instead, get your pillow and punch it hard or hit it against your chair or bed. Avoid hitting things that can hurt you physically like walls. Also, be sober enough not to cause serious damages in your house. It's funny I am telling you all this common sense stuff now but you would be surprised at how necessary it really is.

If you like writing, grab a piece of paper and a pen, write down the hate or range you are feeling. Describe how hurt you are, or how afraid you are. Don't be afraid of the feeling. Let it posses you as you write it down.

When releasing your emotions, it is important to concentrate on the emotion itself and not what caused it. Forget about who did what made you angry and concentrate on 'I hate' or 'I'm so hurt.' Remember, it is the emotion you want to release rather than what caused the emotion.

Speak the truth to release emotions

Sometimes, the emotions buried in us could be released if only we can disclose what happened. Consider telling one person you trust about the event, explain your feeling about the situation, and tell this person how such feelings are affecting you today. I remember one day I was talking to some friends, just banter, nothing of real importance. I made a remark I should maybe have not said and the wrong person overheard and interjected. What they said was hurtful because there was some truth to it. It really made me question my character. I felt so bad for so long until I ran into the person again and we talked over it. Doing this will not only make you feel better for getting whatever it is off your chest, it will also strengthen the relationship you have with the person you are telling.

Sometimes people hide what happened to them because it could be shameful, or if other people know what happened you could be perceived as a bad person. Sharing the story with someone you trust will give you a better perspective of the situation. If you go sharing it with everyone, thinking about the situation over and over again, it will become resentful, this is another problem that should be avoided.

CHAPTER 3: TAKE YOUR EMOTIONAL INTELLIGENCE TO A NEW LEVEL

In this chapter, we will focus on how we can improve the key areas of emotional intelligence (EQ), including self-awareness, self-management, social awareness and relationship management skills.

Self-awareness

You can get a master's degree from various learning institutions but do you know any institution that offers even a bachelor's degree in "You?" I mean an institution where you can learn about yourself. You are one unique subject and if you can be understood at the equivalent master's level, you have the greatest potential to impact your long-term success and happiness.

Many will tell you the journey to a successful life starts with understanding yourself, and they would be right in saying this. Personal growth is all about creating an awareness of your inner self and connecting with your emotions. Psychologists have often said that self-awareness is the ultimate strategy to use in your efforts to control your emotions. This is the one thing that once you understand how it works, you can change your life completely for the better.

Studies have shown that most of the failures in life come from the fact that you let your emotions control your actions. However, if you carefully take your time to identify and analyze the different emotions you face in diverse situations, then you have a chance to free yourself from this prison.

Have you ever seen yourself as a complex system controlled by emotions? The truth is that you are a system whose actions are determined by how well you have learned to control your feelings. The key here is for you to learn what affects your actions and how you respond to different scenarios. We will go into this in greater detail.

How well do you know yourself?

Self-awareness is the ability to understand your behaviors, personality, motivation, thoughts, and emotional reaction processes. According to Daniel Goleman, the author of Emotional Intelligence (published first in 1995) self-awareness is the first capability of having emotional intelligence. Other domains in emotional intelligence are self-regulation, social awareness, and relationship management.

Self-awareness will not only enable you to make sound decisions but also to understand your reactions to others. With that, it is clear that self-awareness is part of emotional intelligence and to achieve a high level of emotional intelligence, you have to be aware of yourself.

Did you know that even sportsmen and women go through an intensive training to understand their emotions before going for competitions? They do this because they need to be aware of all their strengths and weaknesses. Having this type of awareness will then help them to control their actions that are manifested in how they well or bad they play.

Confidence comes as a result of having an assertive conscious mind. You should evaluate how emotions control you when making decisions. Become more self-aware by making a mental note or even writing it down on your phone or piece of paper. Once you have this capability, it will be much easier for you to have justifications for the actions you take in life. When questioned you will be able to give a clear definite answer as to why you took the action you did. You can be sure it was the right decision through applying the appropriate filters of self-awareness.

While trying to understand yourself, there are three necessary steps that you need to know. Firstly, you need to enhance your emotional self-awareness, as it will enable you to recognize your emotions and how they affect your life. Secondly, you should learn how to assess yourself accurately. This will involve identifying your strengths and weaknesses. Grab a pen and some paper or on your laptop make a list of them. Lastly, self-confidence is essential, and you need to cultivate this for you to be aware of yourself.

Developing self-awareness

Can self-awareness be developed? Yes, it can. Set aside some time to analyze yourself and identify the areas you need to develop. Make an effort to strengthen your inner self by employing the measures you deem necessary.

So, how can you spot the areas you need to strengthen? First, allow yourself to know both your strengths and weaknesses. Also, you can consider asking other people such as your friends and relatives to give honest feedback about your strengths and weaknesses. Another way of identifying your strengths or weaknesses is by completing a formal assessment test, which could include a skills test, personality test or test evaluating your abilities.

Once you are aware of your emotional strengths and weaknesses, it will be easy to devise ways of handling your emotional weaknesses while utilizing your emotional strengths to build confidence.

It is important to understand that your values, assumptions, and beliefs also have a direct impact on developing self-awareness. Values are your standards, principles, ethics, morals, and ideas that guide your life. With that, understanding your values is like following a clear road. You will be secure and comfortable because you already know who you are and where you are heading. This will create confidence; you will almost always feel relaxed and happy.

Understanding your assumptions is a significant step towards taking your emotional intelligence to another level. Recall our discussion on emotions in chapter 2, that ignoring emotions hurts our emotional intelligence. Therefore, if you become aware of yourself, it means that you will no longer ignore the assumptions you hold about yourself.

Note that the assumptions you have regarding your life could be either positive or negative. Examples of positive assumptions 'I will be successful,' or 'friends are inherently good.' On the other hand, examples of negative assumptions are 'worse things always happen to me,' or 'I am unable to run a business effectively.'

Self-management

The journey of deconstructing your emotional intelligence can be quite a challenge, for this reason you need the power of self-management to guide you through the process. When you understand your emotions and the impact they have on your daily life, you can progress to this other area of self-management. Note that self-management is built on self-awareness and this implies that you should have the right information regarding your inner self for you to progress.

Self-management requires you to use every detail you have regarding your emotions. You need to do this in such a way as to create positive relationships with others and motivate yourself in every situation.

Creating a positive environment has been proven to be the most powerful strategy in all life expeditions. You can do this by using all the information you have gathered about your emotions to develop positive surroundings. Everyone needs motivation in life, and this is what keeps you going even when you find yourself in bad situations.

You will find that self-management is an essential quality especially in organizations that require their employees to create teams to work together on big projects. You don't want to find yourself in a situation where your emotions are controlling you, and you result in having conflicts with your colleagues.

I appreciate the fact that no one is perfect in this world, but this does not mean that we should allow emotions such as anger to overwhelm us to the point that we can't perform according to the organizational requirements. Instead, we should manage our emotions.

Self-management does not imply that you should never get angry or experience any other emotion towards various situations. There are numerous situations in which anger is the obvious response. The most important thing is not showing everyone that you are angry. Your response to anger should be geared towards resolving the problem at hand. It is always better to proceed with a clear and level head. Your co workers will notice this when the steaks are high and they will look up to you for it. You will have created more value for yourself and the business scenario you find yourself in.

Your assumptions about other people also play a major role in the self-management process. A positive working environment is established by how you and the people around you make assumptions about each other. Never let weird responses to emotions take control of your actions and decisions. Being a victim of this demon will lead you to undesirable behaviors such as criticism, blaming others, focusing on the negative side, thinking on absolutes, foreshadowing, and being influenced by other people. Always ensure that your responses to emotions are inclined towards resolving the conflict.

To practice self-management, look to the following steps.

Start by determining how you feel towards a certain situation. The feeling could be unease about a meeting, loneliness, fear, or even a feeling that there could be something wrong with the environment where you are working. Before you respond to the feeling, you need to exercise self-awareness.

The second thing to do is to carefully and honestly identify the root cause of the emotion. You will need to do an analysis and deep evaluation of the feeling. This appears to be the most difficult step, but it is worth it. For example, if you are a sales person and you have missed a target, are you angry because the marketing department gave you fewer resources or is it because your boss made resentful remarks about the missed target?

Once you identify the feeling and determine its cause, you can now take an action. This action could be as simple as recognizing that you had an inappropriate or unjustified feeling, or that the feeling was directed to the wrong target.

It is important to understand that it is only after we identify the truth behind the causes of our emotions will we be able to manage them even when we are angry or stressed. In every aspect of our lives, be it our work, family, friends, or any other, the concept of self-management is crucial.

The key to self-management, especially when it comes to emotions, lies in how honest you are in appraising your emotions. Whenever you find that you are developing a negative emotion, acknowledge the emotion and accept the fact that you have it, it cannot be changed. Instead of burying it in your soul and pretending that everything is okay, find a sound response to the emotion.

Social-awareness

While developing your emotional intelligence, you need to assess and plan for your social competency. As mentioned in the first chapter, social competency consists of two major parts: relationship management and social awareness.

It is clear that for you to understand other people's emotions, you need first to understand and manage your emotions. Therefore, social awareness can be perceived as an expansion of our self-awareness. For you to be socially aware, you need to develop empathy, service orientation, and organizational awareness.

The greatest benefit of developing social awareness is that it enables you to read situations and people accurately as you are able to understand and empathize with their emotions. Keep in mind that at any workplace or anywhere else, it is good to be able to understand and empathize with what others feel. If you have an unclear understanding of other people in the workplace or home, it is impossible to relate well with them.

When it comes to business, the ability to empathize with others is an important quality for a manager. This value enables the manager to understand and appreciate his employees' emotions.

Furthermore, it is important to note that some factors tend to hinder us from empathizing with others. These could be non-active listening, egocentrism, not recognizing emotional boundaries, and results orientation.

It is an undeniable fact that humans are self-oriented and usually aim at imposing their views on others. Moreover, they tend to think that those around them should act like them. However, this attitude is detrimental when it comes to interacting with others at your place of work. Therefore, you must find ways of achieving your goals while taking into account the various emotions, attitudes, and capabilities of your colleagues to achieve the target.

You can't afford to be self-centered especially in your workplace or even at home. If you are a business manager, you may need to persuade your workforce to perform additional tasks or to rework tasks due to reasons that may be beyond your control. In such situations, the way you communicate with those who report to you should reveal that you empathize with their feelings regarding the request but at the same time, you have to ensure that the task is completed and to the correct standard.

It is wise to reflect on the words as well as body language used during the exchanges to appreciate how your request was reacted to and received. From such findings, you find a style of communication that can effectively convince your team without offending their emotions.

For you to empathize with other people's emotions, you need to listen actively to your communication. With that, you will be able to single out and suspend any prejudgment you have towards the other person's views and empathize with their emotions.

To become an active listener, you need to be focused on whatever you are discussing with others, show them you are listening, acknowledge the other person's views, avoid interrupting when someone is speaking and give an honest and objective response. In any social setting, even at the workplace, your behavior must show that you give your full attention to whoever is speaking by ignoring any mental or environmental distractions.

To achieve an effective social awareness, you should also be aware of various emotional boundaries that you are likely to encounter in your workplace. This implies that you need to distinguish where your emotions end and where other people's emotions start.

Note that you should recognize and feel the feelings of others but not adopt how they feel. Adopting other people's emotions will make you unhappy and keep you on toes while trying to fit yourself in other people's emotions. At worst, adopting someone's emotions will instill fear of giving your views.

The key to understanding emotional boundaries is becoming responsible for your emotions and not other people's emotions. It can be difficult to empathize with others if you don't feel that their emotions are valid in the prevailing circumstances. Therefore, you need to carefully select your responses to acknowledge other people's emotions without necessarily adopting them.

The ability to understand the structure and working of your organization is the second part of social awareness. According to Goleman in his book Primal Leadership (2002), organizational awareness is the ability to understand the structure of your organization, its operational processes, and how various goals are achieved informally in the organization. It involves recognizing the key power of relationships and understanding the organizational culture and values. This implies that organizational awareness is the ability to understand your vendors and clients, comprehend your organization's objectives and operations, then, make decisions with your customers' best interest in mind.

Identifying the key power relationships involves accurately recognizing people who have political influence and power in your organization. Find out who influences the decision-making process, who has the power to give the last node, who gives advice to who, and the significant personal relationships between the people who seem to be more influential in your organization. Note that this level of knowledge about your organization is not for a high emotional intelligence; you should step ahead and learn your organization's culture and value to understand its workings.

To get this information, you need to interact with the organization's vendors and clients. Also, dig deeper into the organization's history, its annual reposts, and what it says on its website to learn more about it. However, sometimes there could be a discrepancy between what is happening and what the organization is saying about itself. With that, you should analyze critically the information you get regarding the organization.

The final area of emotional intelligence, social awareness, is service oriented. Once you understand and empathize with other people's circumstances, including influences in the organization, you will be able to understand their real needs. This information will help you to serve the people in a way that suits their best interests.

If you are a business manager, this is the level of emotional understanding that you should have to ensure that your team is always motivated. This is the reason the appraisal is an important aspect of successful management.

Keep in mind that in any organization, everyone wants his or her efforts to be truly appreciated and valued. Once those who report to you realize that you are appreciating and valuing their efforts, they will be motivated and satisfied.

Always remember that understanding other people's feelings is one of the keys to emotional intelligence. Regardless of whoever you are interacting with, be it colleagues at work or your family at home, if you appear not to be understanding the emotions of those around you, you will be perceived as uncaring and insensitive.

More tips to help you enhance your emotional intelligence

Focus on your emotions each day

You need to identify all the different emotions that you develop in all the diverse situations you face daily. By doing this, you will have a huge set of information to use when making decisions or before you commit to an action. So whenever an emotion comes up, you can determine why you are facing it and how not to let it take control of you.

Use the power of Gestures

Studies show that body language can be used to pass very important messages. You could argue that body language is as effective as verbal communication. The tones, pauses, and pace that you use in communicating with others are affected by emotions. It is, therefore, essential that you focus on your body language skills so as to not get lost or confused. The same applies when you are processing information from other people. Ensure that you correctly translate the gestures into a better emotional intelligence experience.

Be Patient and Understanding

You should learn how to show empathy to others. Sharing your emotions with other people will help you better understand what other people think of you. In this process, you will discover new aspects and dimensions in your consciousness. Be careful not to confuse empathy with sympathy, this is evident when you start feeling for someone rather than feeling with someone. So be patient and allow yourself to first feel your thoughts and then the emotions of other people for a more honest emotional intelligence session.

Self-Examine Yourself

For you to have a better understanding of how emotional intelligence works, you will need to go beyond the basics. Self-regulation is a strategy that is widely used to explore new emotions and to dig deep to the actual causes of each. On top of the basic routines, try new practices and mechanisms that you can use in controlling your emotions.

Be Social

Socializing is hard coded into the brains of many creatures on earth, even animals socialize! Humans need to connect with each other when they interact. You should aim to get as much as possible out of each interaction session. Some of the skills to use here are listening, collaboration, negotiation and being more engaging in conversations. This will help you perfect your social skills and develop emotional intelligence.

These strategies look simple but what you don't know is the potential they have in shaping your emotional intelligence. You can use them in the workplace, at school, and more importantly at home where you get to connect with people close to you. The results will be a more positive self-management experience, self-awareness, and an excellent EQ.

CHAPTER 4: MANAGEMENT AND MOTIVATION

Emotional intelligence is as valuable as the intellectual quotient in the workplace. Traditionally, portraying soft skills was dismissed as being irrelevant and perceived to be unprofessional. However, times have changed, and emotional intelligence is now being recognized as an essential aspect of leadership, governing behavior, influencing relationships, and affecting performance.

Using your emotional intelligence

The ability to be perceptively in tune with your emotions and living with a sound situational awareness is a powerful tool of reshaping your life. You can use it to build lasting business relationships, work-related relationships, and social relationships.

Building Rapport

Don't be surprised that most people have been taught to ignore their emotions and the emotions of coworkers. Most of them believe that being an Archie Bunker-type of a leader is effective leadership, a reason they yell at those who report to them. If you fall in this category, you are going to have a hard time interacting with other people.

Research conducted on emotional intelligence has proved that Archie's approach is not an effective way to get the best outcome in today's business. The only way to build lasting business relationships and achieve success is by understanding other people's emotions, needs and acting in a way that motivates while ensuring that you are benefiting from the relationships.

Use these connective communication skills to build rapport and trust.

1. Learn your team members' expectations

Find out what motivates your team members – advancement, money, or challenge? Whatever motivates them is a legitimate expectation, but you need to know what it is to connect with a team effectively. This will give you an idea regarding what works and what doesn't work when it comes to making work related relationships.

2. Focus more on 'we'

When establishing relationships, it is not all about 'me.' Please note that there are no successful lone rangers. Otherwise, like TV commentator Hugh Downs puts it, "saying that my fate is not tied to yours implies that your end of the boat is sinking."

3. Communicate personally

Sometimes, ineffective managers tend to hide behind electronic forms of communication to avoid genuine human contact. These are the people who will email a coworker seated 20 feet away instead of going to talk to them face to face. Karl Albrecht, the Aldi supermarket chain founders, once observed that making things happen involves making people respect you, like you, and desire to connect with you. Keep in mind that human connection usually outranks the digital connection.

4. Become an active listener

As said earlier, active listening is very important when it comes to social awareness. Avoid distractions as much as you can especially when listening to someone. Consider putting your phone down and eliminating anything that can distract you.

You need to use your emotional intelligence skills to build rapport and trust in your place of work, business world, and even in your social relationships. Understand other people's emotions, listen to them, empathize with their emotions, and put their needs ahead of yours. With that, you will succeed in building stronger relationships.

Optimism

Emotional intelligence can also help you to build optimism and live a positive life. If we can learn optimism, why is pessimism so common? Do we have any control over our attitudes or do we just live the way we are?

Henry Ford once said that "If you think you can do a thing, or you think you can't do a thing– you are right." this rings true with research in neuroscience that revealed that optimists are individuals whose brains bias is towards optimism while pessimists are individuals who tend view situations through a lens of pessimism. While this sounds very obvious I think this is important to draw attention to. It's just an attitude, a lens, a way of looking at things. You don't have to think for very long to realize what attitude you need to adopt if you want to be happy in life. You would be right if you said optimism. After some time, pessimism may be hard wired into the brain. The person wanting to change their outlook on situations and life as a whole must make a conscious effort to change their ways.

It is worth noting that reality is objective in the two types of situations described. Your reality is real to you. However, life features both pessimism and optimism, and sometimes you can get what you want, or you don't. What storyline or meaning do you attach to the outcomes you encounter?

The choice of stress or happiness, being overwhelmed, it's within your control, whether pessimism was learnt or genetic, you have the ability to change it. Enhanced self-awareness and self-management are strong foundations of emotional intelligence and are also building blocks of optimism and resiliency.

To be an optimist, you need to be aware of what's going on around you and direct your attention towards finding a solution to the complex equation you may be facing instead of focusing on the threats or disappointments accompanying the current or past situation. The way you direct your attention towards situations forms your perception of reality. This is the reason optimists see potential positive realities while pessimists see negative realities.

It is important to be mindful of how we direct our focus of attention. Optimism protects us from depression, hopelessness, and powerlessness. These are factors that ignite and fire up stress, a condition we all know it is detrimental to our health.

Use emotional intelligence to manage conflicts

Exercise: Answer this question correctly.

Conflict in the workplace is____

a) Preventable

b) Necessary

c) Avoidable

d) All of the above

If you are afraid of conflicts, you must have rushed to (a). However, (d) is the right answer. Conflicts are bound to occur in organizations, and this is natural and expected. The most important thing is to learn how to respond to these conflicts without negatively affecting other people.

Taking time to evaluate a conflict enables you to understand its power to transform the current situation. You will also be able to single out the cause of the conflict, understand the other party's emotions regarding the conflict, and device a way of responding to the conflict effectively.

Failure to analyze a conflict could result in the wrong reaction to the wrong cause and worst cases tear down our relationship with workmates or even with friends and family. This will result in reduced morale and has a negative impact on your performance at your workplace. Also, it can reduce productivity, encourage absenteeism, and in the worst case, foster violence or aggression.

The first step in using emotional intelligence while handling a conflict at the place of work is to avoid the wrong response to the situation. Avoid anger at all costs because bursting with a range in front of someone you share an unresolved conflict is like bleeding and falling in water inhabited by sharks. However, staying calm and analyzing the situation well will help you to make a sound decision.

Sometimes, you could be doing something wrong to the other party, but you are not aware. By practicing social-awareness, you can avoid such conflicts or solve them in a better way rather than yell at each other.

Note that conflict management is about respect, teamwork, collaboration, flexibility, and negotiations. People with high emotional intelligence tend to be good in conflict management because they use self-awareness, self-management, social awareness and relationship management skills to solve conflicts.

CHAPTER 5: IMPROVE YOUR EMOTIONAL HEALTH

Do you care about your emotional well-being and act effectively when you knock yourself on a rough patch? Please, let's be honest here, the majority of us don't. Let's assume that you pay attention to your psychological well-being. Are you aware of the strategies you can use to ease emotional pain especially when you get hurt? Would you know how to boost your confidence when a situation lowers your self-esteem? Or do you know how you should recover after you encounter a loss? The answer is the same – most of us don't!

This is a surprising truth and a convenient one as well because our emotional well-being has a direct impact on our quality of life just like our physical health. Even when we note our general emotional harm, we do nothing regarding emotional maintenance. Let's perform a comparison between how you react to sprains, coldness, cuts, etc. and our emotional health. We always rush for sweaters and gulp down warm chicken soup to keep a cold at bay, bandage cuts, and apply ice packs to sprains. What about our emotional health? We do nothing! Mainly because a lot of us are ignorant to the fact and not many people or institutions will tell you that.

When it comes to getting care and attention, our emotional health requires us to do a lot of catching up. A good method to start closing this gap is to 'treat' the common psychological 'sprains, cuts and burns' whenever we sustain them. Here are some tips to help you.

Guard your self-esteem

Self-esteem can be perceived as the armor that you wear to the 'life battle,' and when it's low, you tend to become self-critical and harm your self-esteem further. One thing I'm sure is that you can't apply salt on a cut or go jogging in a sleeveless T-shirt in freezing weather if you had a cold, but for a reason, I don't know, you have no qualms about kicking your self-esteem.

Weak self-esteem exposes you to vulnerable situations such as rejection, failure, stress, and anxiety. Therefore, you need to practice self-compassion especially when your self-esteem is low, and stop self-criticism. If self-critical thought attacks your mind, think of how you would react to a friend who expressed such feelings. Then, address those thoughts to yourself. Self-compassion will help your self-esteem to recover and enhance your emotional health.

Gain control after failure

Failure has a negative impact on our perceptions and disorients us in such a way that our objectives seem far beyond our reach and our abilities appear to be less. This results in helplessness and loss of motivation.

Whenever you encounter failure, instead of complaining and perceiving yourself as incompetent, use your emotional intelligence to review your objectives and the approach you used. List down all the factors that you can control. This may include planning, preparation and efforts, then, think of how you can enhance your execution of each of the plans.

Focusing on what you can control will balance the negative thoughts, enhance your motivation, and significantly increase the chances for your future success.

Avoid brooding thoughts at all costs

Stewing over annoying events will keep us feeling worse as brooding thoughts are detrimental to our emotional health. When you notice that you are stuck in the cycle of such thoughts, disrupt the urge of worrying by developing a zero tolerance attitude towards the distressing thoughts and immerse yourself in the now. Think of all the things you have going for you and that at any moment it could all change if you want it to. Control your thoughts to the ones that are going to be most profitable to you. If you find yourself doing otherwise, this is good as you're developing self-awareness. Once you are aware of a detrimental thought you could act internally to remedy the situation. Mantras are often beneficial in this type of situation i.e. verbally reassuring yourself.

Regain your self-worth after rejection

Rejections register in our brains like physical pain, and this is the reason they are so painful. Unless you realize that, you are likely to misinterpret the magnitude of psychological pain you feel as an indication that you are needy, weak or pathetic, and this can damage your self-worth. It is also worth noting that people are sensitive to this in varying levels of intensity. Some mentally strong people will simply not be affected by rejection in ways that others are. There is truly a diverse pallet in which to observe this behavior.

If you are someone that is affected heavily by rejection, remind yourself of what you can offer. List down all the attributes you possess and maintain you are very useful in the area in which you were rejected. Doing this will ease your emotional pain, help you to recover your self-worth, and enhance your emotional health.

Emotional health and well being make up a major part of your life, for this reason you should ensure that your emotional health is in a good state. The habits previously discussed in this chapter will help you to maintain good emotional health if you are consistent in applying them.

Conclusion

Congratulations on reading through this piece! I hope you've learned a lot. You will now have a better understanding of this very subjective set of experiences, and the tools you need to make sense of it all. Through the medium of improving your self-awareness, self-management, social awareness, and relationship management skills, you will be able to positively influence your life. Furthermore, understanding the emotional impacts of blame and the importance of personal accountability will help you to understand yourself and as you excel in your profession. I really cannot put enough emphasis on the importance of understanding your personal nature and your tendencies. Once you can get a solid understanding of this, as mentioned previously, you will be in good standing to manage your emotions appropriately when they arise.

Not only will this information have influence on your family relationships, if applied correctly, you will also put yourself in a higher standing in the workplace. Furthermore, professional and personal success in diverse organizations relies on one's ability to understand and express emotions; as well as responding to the emotions of people we work with – empathy. Once you can empathize with your co-workers or perhaps the people who work under you, you will get a lot more respect in the workplace. This will open the door to a range of new experiences and really help the team to synergize; as a result the working environment will appear to be increasingly pleasant.

Conclusion

Thank you again for downloading this book!

I hope this book was able to help you gain a better understanding of emotional intelligence.

Please continue reading as I have included another one of my titles, 'Mental Toughness' as a free bonus!

Finally, if you enjoyed this book, then I'd like to ask you for a favor, would you be kind enough to leave a review for this book on Amazon? It'd be greatly appreciated!

Click here to leave a review for this book on Amazon!

Here Is Your Free Book!

Mental Toughness:
Apply These Simple Techniques To Improve Your Mental Toughness

T.G. Benfield

INTRODUCTION
More to it than meets the Eye

What is it that makes a good athlete, good parent or good leader? Why is it that some people accomplish their goals, while others try, but eventually end up failing? What is the cause? We all have our explanations and invariably end up talking about the talent of top performers in their respective fields. Take for example someone who happens to be the smartest scientist in a lab, or the fastest person in the team. Another person could be a brilliant business strategist. Is natural talent all there is? Or is there more to it than meets the eye? Intelligence and inherent talent will only take you so far on the path to success.

Grit, Tenacity and Perseverance

Talking of research, it is said that intelligence and inherent talent account for only 30% of what you achieve overall. The research points out that your grit, tenacity or mental toughness plays a far more important role, above all else in achieving your goals. Be it in the areas of health, sport, business or life. As it accounts for a major chunk of what is to determine your eventual success in any field, you must be wondering whether it is genetic? Fortunately for you it is beyond genetics, unlike inborn talent or innate intelligence. This factor suggests that you can develop grit over time through constructive habit forming.

Vital Ingredient for Success

There is hardly anything you can do about altering the composition of the genes you were born with. However, one can surely develop their mental fitness by adopting a slew of measures, detailed in this book. To begin the process, try stretching the very limits of your physical, mental and emotional capacities. One would certainly be inclined to think, that the ones who happen to be bigger, stronger and seemingly intelligent would be the ones who are going to score better and come out with flying colors. Well that is only partly correct.

Table of contents:

CHAPTER 1: DEVELOP MENTAL TOUGHNESS
What is mental toughness?

Mental toughness entails partaking in the psychosomatic edge that permits one to accomplish at peak extreme effort and efficiency throughout the strains that are placed on them during competition, training, interactions, and internal dialogue. Specifically, when the strains are extreme or the situations become opposing. At any time, the demands are the greatest when the features of mental toughness are the most obvious.

Three secrets in developing mental toughness were recently revealed by a former Navy SEAL and Navy SEAL instructor, Phil Black. These closely guarded secrets will lead you to develop greater levels of mental toughness and to dominate your game and workout. They are easy to practice while also being highly effective and are used by some of the most elite athletes on this planet.

There are many aspects of mental toughness and mental training, but the principles are simple and can be rooted down into a few main components. It doesn't matter if it's for sports like baseball, basketball, tennis or boxing. Alternatively, for fitness like running, weight lifting, or martial arts. These principles of mental fitness, the psychology of it, can be applied in any area.

First, what is mental toughness? Mental toughness is the ability to persist during events that go wrong, are difficult and/or strenuous. It is the ability to keep your internal dialogue (your self-talk) positive despite negative external occurrences.

From when you were born until the age of 18, you were told "no" 150,000 times. That is 700 times a month or 22 times a day! People tell you, "No, get away from there" and "Stop doing that". Some of these were to prevent you from danger, some to prevent you growing because of other people's fears or ignorance.

This causes you to be highly susceptible to negative influence. Psychologists have found that 77% or internal self-talk is negative and counteracting. Now do you realize how much of our potential is being held back?

I know you have likely heard that there are no limits on what we can be, have and do. This statistic shows pretty clearly that we are the ones that hold ourselves back more than anything else does!

Therefore, you must control your mind or "they" will do it for you. This is how Navy SEALs have done it:

Monitor your self-talk, that internal dialogue of what you are telling yourself every day. Become a watcher of your mind. Do you have positive thoughts or negative thoughts? What are you feeling like on a day-to-day and moment-to-moment basis? Are you adding to the negative side or the positive side? For two days, write everything down that is negative, for 48 hours. Just your negative thoughts, you want to become aware of how much of what you think is negative. Remember, psychologists found that on average 77% or your internal talk is negative, what percent is yours?

Filter out negative events and thoughts. What kind of material do you read? What type of people do you hang out with? How often do you laugh with those around you? That is an indicator of how well things are going. Become purposeful about what you let into your mind, put on a filter and screen out negative influences. Your environment, the people you associate, and the things you read or listen to are big influences on the way you think. In a positive environment, it is much easier to weather any storm that comes.

Reframe all negative events in a positive light. Use your sense of humor and your brain will encode it differently. Just because something is negative, doesn't mean that you have to accept it that way. Much of life is how you respond to it. If your training is difficult and demanding, you could say, "Ha! Ha! This workout is killing me, is this all there is? I want some more, I'm just warming up. I'm tougher than all of this, you can't defeat me!"

CHAPTER 2: GET ENOUGH SLEEP

Sleep and rest is a vital component of any athlete's training program. A performance athlete for example, wants to be able to work harder and excel to set new records. It is imperative they pay attention to their sleeping habits - extra hours of sleep overnight translates to better performance in training sessions and in competition.

It's a balancing act, getting enough sleep each night between training sessions so they're recovered enough to have a quality workout the next day. Balance is the secret of successful training, especially if you're a young athlete. In my experience, far too few student-athletes make the time for adequate sleep.

Professional trainers and coaches know studies have confirmed athletes perform at higher levels when they get extra sleep. Generally, competitive athletes who get an extra two hours of quality sleep a night consistently, instead of the usual eight hours, are better prepared both physically and mentally for peak performance.

Olympic level athletes often take ten or more hours of sleep a night during training. They know by their results the importance of being well rested to improve their performance during competitions. The best athletes understand getting enough rest between their training sessions is just as important as getting a little extra sleep the night before a competitive event.

Getting extra sleep offers benefits in these areas:

1) Increased energy, available to allow you to "dig deep" when necessary.

2) Improved mood, including during competition and a feeling of readiness.

3) Decreased fatigue after exertion and quicker recovery - important for events requiring short bursts such as football and soccer.

4) Increased mental acuity.

5) A lower risk of injuries due to fatigue

So now you know this, it's easy to change your athlete's sleeping regime to get more, right?

Well, I know it isn't. There are many competing demands on high school athlete's time these days. Student athletes are already busy with school and practice and it can be tough to find the time for extra sleep. In many cases, only the advice of their personal trainer or coach will give a young athlete the motivation they need to make extra sleep a part of their training schedule.

While getting an extra two hours a night sleep isn't going to turn everybody into a Division 1 college athlete, not getting enough can certainly ruin any chances of achieving the best you can be! Additionally, getting too little sleep can lead to all manner of medical and mental problems such as lack of confidence and motivation. So a lack of sleep has detrimental effects on physical, mental and emotional health. Adequate sleep allows athletes to be rested and energetic for workouts while reducing the risk of injuries.

An athlete who fails to get the sleep they need finds their performance beginning to slip - by contrast, none of the studies, which have been conducted on the effects of extra sleep on athletic performance, have indicated any negative effects.

Appropriate preparation is the key to success for any sport and one of these preparations is being well rested before training sessions and not just for competition. Extra sleep is a serious matter for young and student-athletes and is one more thing they can do to reach their peak performance. Not only is this information applicable to student athletes, but also to the wider population who dream of achieving big things in areas other than sport.

CHAPTER 3: EMBRACING CHANGE

Everyone engages in some bad practices. Various people smoke, several binge eat and a number may even engage in self-destructive behavior. These habits are often deeply ingrained into one's personality, to the point of becoming the traits by which many define themselves. If you want to change the course of your life you have to learn how to change these habits first. Although it is often a long and difficult process, the results will allow you to succeed where you may have otherwise failed. The steps below can help you learn how to identify, confront and eventually eliminate the detrimental habits that may control your life.

Changing Your Habits

Like muscles, habits also get stronger every time you exercise them. Your bad habits are often part of who you are. You might make excuses for them, embrace them or even get a bit prickly when others bring them up. In reality though, these are not just habits -- they are a failing mechanism. They might be holding you back from accomplishing success in business, your social life or even love. Embracing your bad habits means simply learning how to live with what is going wrong and becoming more aware, but eliminating them means that you are willing to make a positive change in your own life. There is nothing that says this is easy, of course, but you should be willing to try it. After all, getting rid of your bad habits is one of the few ways that you can take control of your own life.

What Does It Mean To Get Rid of Bad Habits?

Getting rid of bad habits is more than just eliminating a negative behavior. To truly rid yourself of a bad habit you have to learn how to make effective changes in your life. If you fail to do so you might replace your current bad habit with one that is just as bad. Or worse, you might even find yourself slipping back into old habits without giving yourself a chance to change. Instead, you must consider breaking bad habits to be a journey that will allow you to understand not only what you are doing wrong, but also why you have made the choices you have made. While this is not always a pleasant experience it can help you to change your life for the better. The benefits of doing such a thing are often realized with time, you're then wishing you made these changes sooner as time is valuable and stops for no man.

How To Make A Change

The process of changing bad habits is as follows. The first, and perhaps most important step, is to figure out why you do what you do. Take the time to log your bad habits, noting both the time and what preceded the action. If your bad habit is late-night snacking, try to get an idea of the situation in which it occurs. Do you snack because you are hungry, or because you are stressed? If you know why you undertake the behavior you are more likely to be able to change it.

After you figure out the "why" you can move on to making a change. Sometimes, the mere knowledge of the behavior will be enough to break the habit. For others, it will take greater discipline. Try giving yourself a small reward when you go a day without performing the habit. Or try to take time to replace the bad habit with something positive. If you like to smoke in the morning, for example, you might be better served by going for a run. Changing the behavior is a key to controlling your life.

What Happens After The Change?

The real question when making any kind of life change is whether the effort is worth it. For most, eliminating a bad habit can have one of many possible side effects. You might eliminate a habit that costs you money, or you might eliminate something that allows you a better chance to excel at work. You might become more attractive to the opposite sex in some cases and you might learn to have a better opinion of yourself in others. No matter the specific change, though, you will be engaging in a process that will allow you to have greater control of your own life. You may think that you are only eliminating a problem habit, but the reality of the situation is that you are taking the first steps on a path to greater personal success.

Chapter 4: Accepting Failure

A Chinese proverb says, "The great question is not whether you have failed, but whether you are content with failure."

It is said that before you can succeed, you must fail. You should accept that and learn from it. New opportunities can come from failure. Don't brush aside your failures, take a look at them and try to figure what it was that caused you to fail. Was it something you didn't do, or maybe something you did that you shouldn't have? Ask someone you respect why they think you may have failed.

Look for the opportunities that may present themselves in your failures. Have the courage to go after the new opportunities that occur from your failures.

Do not avoid failure; use your failures as a stepping-stone to success. You need those failures in order to succeed. Stop letting failure have a negative hold on your thoughts and emotions.

It is said that the more we fail, the more we succeed. With that in mind, our failures are needed so we can get closer to success. It is okay to fail, as long as we do something with those failures. Have the courage to face your failures and make the most of them. Courage is not something that comes easy for a lot of people.

Life is full of failures and rejections. People who constantly complain or give up altogether are destined to live disappointing lives. Those who take action and find creative solutions to their disappointments and challenges are successful in the end. Their compensation is the life of their dreams. If you're not aiming for something specific, measurable and defined, you may end up somewhere else.

The way you see yourself is the way you project yourself to others. If you do not contemplate you can succeed, then you probably will not. Why would others choose to follow you if you do not think you can succeed?

To be successful, you need to see the positive things in your life. You also need to be confident and happy. You need to appreciate the positive things in your life. Be the forever optimist; always see the glass as half-full, not half empty.

Do not set your goals too low. Make every sweat to be the best at whatever you do and make sure your plans are realistic. Maybe part of the reason for failure is because you have set yourself some unrealistic deadlines. If you are not able to bump into your deadlines, reset your deadlines and go for it.

We all devote too much time focusing on our limitations and weaknesses. We all have weaknesses. We all have strengths too. Discover where your strengths are and focus on them. Ignore the weaknesses and build your life around your strengths. You will have higher self-esteem, a better outlook on life and a better attitude about yourself and life in general.

You were born to do something in this world. Find out what that something is and go after it with everything you have.

Are you ready should an opportunity present itself? Get prepared, so that when it does you can grab onto it and capitalize on it.

Chapter 5: Confidence

Self-confidence can be loosely defined as one's confidence in his/her own abilities, character and worth. It's not uncommon to find people who have very little or even none, of this. If you're one of those people who want to improve on their self-confidence, you have to know that it always starts on the inside. Work out the issues that you have that causes you to have low confidence in the first place. Once you have worked these things out, then you can work on the outside appearances. Here are a few self-confidence tips that will help you to be able to look more confident on the outside.

1. Walk and stand tall. Your presence affects how you look to other people, and whether we like it or not, other people's opinions of us still have an effect on our self-confidence, though it should not depend on it. When you stand and walk tall, you will actually look like you are confident, even during the times that you're not.

2. Try and improve your social skills. When you are more sociable, people tend to talk to you more as opposed to if you were always hiding in some corner just leering at everyone who passes by. Try to talk to people more, have a little chit chat here and there. It never pains to ask someone how they are doing, even in passing. This will show that you are confident enough to put yourself out there for people to talk to. In addition, remember, a genuine smile on your face works better than expensive makeup or clothes.

3. All articles that contain self-confidence tips will agree: you have to be a go-getter. When people see that you are driven to achieve your goals, they will take this as a sign of self-confidence, and will subsequently lead to them respecting you more.

4. Always be prepared! This is especially useful in the workplace. When you are prepared for your work, let's say you have a presentation for your big corporate bosses; you will exude self-confidence because you know what you are talking about. It would be humiliating to be talking in front of very important people and suddenly draw a blank and just start mumbling in front of them. These kinds of situations can crumble your self-esteem. When you are always prepared, you will be able to conquer these fears and speak of the things that you already know like the back of your hand.

5. The most practical of all self-confidence tips is this: work to make your body the way that you want it to be. In the looks department, it's no secret that some people are more fortunate than others. There are those that can eat, eat, and not even gain a pound. If you're not one of these blessed people and you're not happy with how your body looks, then do something about it. There are so many gyms, sports and activities that you can commit to become a better version of yourself. You can try boxing, biking or maybe even take up the art of Wushu. Either way,

when you do something to get your body to the way you want it to look, you will definitely feel better about yourself and your self-confidence will begin to soar.

Everyone deserves to live their dreams, low self-confidence should not be the reason that you don't get to live yours.

CHAPTER 6: DEVELOP SELF-AWARENESS

Self-awareness is the ability of realizing all his or her capabilities and functions, in a leadership role for example. Being aware of who you are through the lens of leadership requires a lot of scrutinizing of yourself. One is constantly aware of the things that you can and cannot do. It also involves your ability to realize how you react to different stimuli as a leader in an organization. A leader should always have a very holistic idea about his or her abilities.

Self-awareness involves asking a variety of questions that are directed towards the personality of the person involved. When you are able to properly identify those key elements of your personality, which come together to make you who you are, then and only then can you say you are fully aware of whom you are. Such elements of ones personality may include things like strengths, weaknesses, thoughts, emotions and beliefs.

In reality, there are certain major areas that must be critically looked at if you are to fully be aware of who you are and what you are capable of doing. These things should always be present in your analysis in order to be sure that you have really taken a very deep and critical look into yourself.

Keep going through the text below and you will, at the end, get to know what areas you need to look at which are responsible for self-awareness.

Emotional self-awareness: This refers to the ability of an individual to realize how he or she reacts to all the things that are related to emotions and capacity as a person. Being able to know how you react when presented with a variety of conditions will help you to develop awareness of your emotions and how they affect the things that you do. Our emotions have a way of affecting our actions, these effects can either be positive or negative depending on how the person concerned tends to react to such situations. It is your duty as a leader and as an individual to take a very holistic look into your emotions. Find out what makes you react angrily so that you can try to avoid such things in the future. Whatever it is that generates a good emotional response within you should be encouraged.

Those things that are known to make you edgy and less friendly to be with should be totally avoided or lasting solutions found to them.

Accurate self-assessment: This involves taking stock of all the things that you are capable of doing and those that you cannot do. This area is mainly concerned with identifying what your fears are and how you tend to deal with those fears. It is also related to how you tend to live your life and the decisions or choices that you make on a daily basis. In trying to accurately assess yourself, you need to be very truthful to yourself so that you will have a clear impression of what really ticks you and what makes you go haywire. Identification of the limits that you can also reach under pressure and your normal performance levels are all included in accurately assessing yourself, which is an essential feature of total self-awareness.

Self-confidence: Being confident in yourself does not mean taking decisions without first trying to find out what will be expected of you. It is more like first finding the depth of a river before jumping in, so that you don't drown when you realize that it is very deep. Confidence is a way of saying that you believe in what you want to do or what you are doing and it is mainly due to the fact that you have really considered everything that relates to the task you want to accomplish. This area tasks you to identify the level of confidence that you do have in your own self and how positive you are of yourself. This will help you realize how committed you will be towards the achievement of the goals that you and the other group members have set in those situations when the going gets tough. Remember, a person with great self-belief is needed to help boost the belief of the others.

These are the three main areas needed in self-awareness creation.

CHAPTER 7: CONFLICTS

When it comes to handling conflicts, I personally think that there is a single skill that can be said to be the most important. The idea of having 'the most important skill' is mind-boggling and sounds weird. Naturally, the ability to handle conflicts-whether to resolve or manage them is a combination of many skills. In a way, it's like asking what the most important ingredient of a cake is. If you've ever baked one you know that there isn't such an ingredient. A good cake requires flour, sugar, eggs, etc. and not only the right ingredients but also the right amount of each. Without the required list and in the right amount we'll get a weird tasteless cake.

Applying the same analogy of baking a cake, conflict handling differs in that there is an ingredient more important than all others. As a matter of fact, this component is quite essential in any process involving change. In that light, conflict resolution is a specific situation of change creation. One needs to convert conflict patterns - whether before if they've become apparent or after they have reached the surface - into a more constructive pattern.

This brings me to the most important conflict handling skill, the art of reflection.

Reflection is one's ability to truly contemplate oneself.

Conflicts are the result of egoic patterns - patterns that come from the mind and which compel us to behave in what I refer to as conflict-prone conduct. For example, the egoic bias of relativism, the tendency to compare one's situation, possession or whatever is currently perceived under scarcity, with another person's situation, who is prone to make one regard the situation at hand as a 'Me vs. You' situation. As you can easily deduce, no collaborative endeavor is possible when such a perception reigns. With that in mind, if you find yourself frowning with the thought "of course it's a Me vs. You situation, after all it IS a conflict we're talking about here..." then you are a perfect proof of the idea I have put forward above. We are so engrossed to the egoic mind patterns to an extent that they literally govern the way we regard, and to a deeper extent, react to conflicts.

Within a pattern, no critical thinking is ever possible. This feature is the essence of any pattern. It serves as a minimal thinking unit and hence does not enable any thinking within it. On one hand, patterns serve as major time savers. We tend to act in a predetermined way without getting entangled in unnecessary thinking. A good example is your ability to drive without having to think of our next action, a phenomena that's quite beneficial. On the other hand, the supposed blessing is in itself a curse since without conscious awareness; the driver will be acting as an autopilot. Thus, in order to create a change in one's course of action, a light must be switched on and the conscience should be awoken. Such a light can only be switched on in the presence of reflection. Only when you truly envisage yourself will you be able to notice the pattern and be able to contain it.

As I highlighted earlier, handling disputes is a definite method of creating a transition. If one is engrossed in the bias of relativism, they will continue fighting the other side, as this is what they perceive as the only way to achieve their goals. When you contemplate your behavior, in the long run, you might discover that clutching onto a Me vs. You mindset doesn't really work to one's advantage, but rather incapacitates it.

There exists one catastrophe though; the reflective ability diminishes around conflicts. This fact helps explain why conflicting parties often act in a way that is clearly not in their best interest and hence are usually unable to stop. During disputes, the power of self-reflection is replaced by a frantic clinging to one's school of thought, with the aim of self-justification. In the absence of self-awareness, discussing proper goal setting, or using communication skills, or any other conflict handling skills are of no benefit since all other conflict handling strategies are relevant only when reflection is present. It is therefore clear at this point that the most important skill in conflict handling and management is reflection.

How can you create reflection when you get entangled in a dispute? The response is simple, just become aware of the signs of the conflict patterns. After which you will realize that you are reacting to the pattern. It is therefore one's responsibility to pay great attention to the conflict pattern, which will induce the process of self-reflection.

Furthermore, Participating in healthy conflicts requires particular personality attributes that permit individuals to interact and share ideas and opinions healthily. It is important that you maintain your sense of alertness and be on the lookout for the tell tale indications of unhealthy conflicts.

A totally free and objective exchange of recommendations, opinions, and suggestions characterize healthy conflicts. Its counterpart, however, may be the exact opposite. Handled tension always prevails throughout the onset of healthy conflicts. If this gets out of hand, members of the conflict are at chance of taking things personally.

Getting defensive and striking back via a personal attack may ensue. Extra criticisms and unfavorable responses or opinions about the project or proposed option are voiced out. Moreover, the dispute may extend past the debate itself. If you see participants who were once on friendly terms begin to ignore each other, this only implies the brewing of a cold war. Thus, it signifies that the conflict has gone overboard and may even deal damage to the whole team unless otherwise addressed immediately.

Dealing with the worsening conflict necessitates your mediation. If you don't step in, the strain may escalate and disrupt the harmonious performing relationship in your team. Considering that healthy conflicts serve to help the organization, from the start, it would be advisable to hire those who are open to conflict and are capable of debating resolutions, if needed. Such employees would boost the importance of your team.

CHAPTER 8: EXERCISE FAIRNESS

It has been a fundamental tradition for a very long time, that a director or a boss of a company had the right to gauge his employees' performance. This was done at the time when the bonus or appraisal was given. At the time, the manager had to select the best employee based on performance. However, this was a good procedure to appraise one's performance with bonus or any promotion.

Nevertheless, later sometimes, this activity showed some glimpse of drawback in the form of partiality done by the manager or head. For example, if the manager had some problem with any employee, then they could directly either fire them or demote them, just to take revenge. Alternatively, if, the manager liked somebody or someone persuaded with buttering, then the promotion or bonus was given to that employee rather than to deserving candidate.

Nevertheless, time has changed a lot, as now; not only the manager, but employees too can give ratings to their head and all this is possible with the help of an innovative and praiseworthy application called "Rate My Boss". This application now enables the employees of any company to give ratings on their head in accordance with some quality statistics, moreover, the other employees of that same company can give their reviews about that rating and their manager.

Therefore, the best part of this application is that, no rating can be impartial, as there are some reviews over any report. For example; if one employee of the company X is giving some rating to his boss through Rate My Boss application, which may be good or bad, nevertheless, if other employees of the same company X give some reviews over that rating, then the original result could be easily drawn from it.

Some qualities that are included under this application are team management skills, communication skills, knowledge, experience, fairness, ability to convey message to employees, flexibility, and optimism. Any employee can give ratings to his manager under these qualities from 1 to 5, i.e. if they are excellent 5 points, worst then, 1. After giving ratings under each quality, an average rating will be generated, that will be shown in the top display. The other employees will see these ratings, then they too can tell that how much the scale is accurate and also, if they too feel the same or not.

This application has now changed the mindsets of both employees and manager, as now the manager too knows, if he does not treat his employees well and exercise fairness, then the result could generate an adverse reaction for him.

CHAPTER 9: SETTING GOALS

Before creating a business plan, before choosing a product, even before developing a marketing technique you need to first consider the basic building blocks. For example if you aim to develop a work from home enterprise. The objectives that are set and achieved will help build the success that you are searching for.

The basics for setting a goal are an open secret known with top-caliber athletes, successful business people and Internet entrepreneurs. Establishing objectives gives you short-term and long-term motivation and focus. These ambitions can help you strive to acquire the knowledge for developing a home-based business or whatever you desire to create. In addition, they aid with organizing your resources and time.

Setting clearly defined short and long term goals for making money online, for example, will help measure your progress and achieve the satisfaction that success creates. Charting your effort will also provide the opportunity for enjoying the stages of completion that lead to the actual realization of the purpose. This eliminates the frustration of a long and pointless grind towards the creation of your home business. Self-confidence will also improve while becoming aware of your capabilities for completing the desired goals.

What do you really hope to accomplish with a home business? After giving this idea some thought, create short and long-term goals for achieving it. Then you have to break down these objectives into smaller, more manageable targets. Once you have developed a list, start immediately.

A good way to manage your list is to create daily, weekly and monthly destinations for developing an Internet business, or whatever endeavor you wish to pursue. This will help you stay focused. Every day will provide an opportunity for fulfilling a certain goal giving you a feeling of accomplishment. As a human it is imperative that you feel as though you are accomplishing and moving forward. Good self-discipline and work ethic will ensure you meet your targets in time.

Here are various thoughts that can help you set goals for creating a home-based enterprise AND for achieving them:

Attitude

Attitude plays a very big role in anything we do in our lives. Does bad perspective hold you back from completing goals? Analyze your self-talk and behavior. What do you hear? What do you see? Do you notice any hindrances that can become obstacles for developing a plan? If you do have complications in these areas then the immediate thing to do is address the situation. A goal begins with your thoughts. Thoughts guide your actions. Strive to improve them.

Time Management

Home-based enterprises are created with the help of good time management. Failing with an online business can be attributed to disorganization. The developmental stages of your home business will require a large amount of time and a great deal of effort. Organizing your time efficiently can help achieve success.

Education

Education is key in achieving your goals. Purpose to become an expert in developing the home business of your choice. If your objectives require specialized knowledge or a certain skill, make plans to obtain the appropriate education. The more tools that you have for creating Internet success, the easier it will be to hit the targets.

Family

This is possibly the most significant element when creating goals for developing a home business. Your family should never be left out of the plans. They are your support and foundation and all of the targets that are developed should flow from a commitment to them. Online ventures come and go but family is forever.

Finances

Finances also play a major role in achieving your goals. Have realistic objectives for the income and expenses that will be incurred with your business. Create a timetable for reaching your earning potential.

Recreation

Do not set the bar at a level that requires a 24/7 effort. Create a goal that will give you some down time at least one day per week. Burnout is a trap that many fall into. Making money online can come easier with a clear head and a rested body. Factor some fun time into your objectives and schedule time away from the office.

Blueprint

It is not a corrupt idea to think big and focus small. Develop your goals by setting a 10-year plan, a 5-year plan and 1-year plan. Then narrow your focus by creating 6-month targets, monthly targets, weekly targets and daily targets. Remember, this is a building process. Each goal that is accomplished is another block in the foundation of your home business success.

Before you begin to make money on the Internet, a foundation must be laid. The building blocks for home business success are the goals that you create and the effort that is made to achieve them. These ideas can help develop the objectives that lead to your achievements.

"Experience tells you what to do; confidence allows you to do it."

CHAPTER 10: SPEAKING UP

If you have an abusive boss, one who criticizes or belittles you, and shows no respect for your abilities or concern for your development, you may decide to hold your tongue, keep your head down, and get along as best you can until you find another position. However, you dread getting up for work every morning.

Alternatively, your sense of outrage may take over and one day you explode in frustration and anger. Afterward, the disciplinary process that you have to undergo and the difficult relationship you have created between you and your manager/boss make what had been a bad situation even worse.

There is a better way! If you follow the steps below you have every chance of creating a conversation that gives you the positive outcome you need.

Consider a situation where you have a very competent manager who has a lot of experience and company service. Your problem is that when you raise an idea of your own, she shoots you down before she has heard more than a few words of what you have to say. You are becoming more and more frustrated and feel that you not being allowed to grow or develop in your job.

You need to speak up, but to do so in a way that does not result in accusation or argument, achieves a change in the behavior of your manager, and enables you to keep your job. When your power base is low, the stakes high, and you want to approach a difficult subject with the least possible risk to your relationship, and your job, proceed with care utilizing the steps below.

Open the conversation by setting a tone that does not accuse, but does signal that something serious is to follow. Avoid getting into any detail at this stage. You can start with a general question or you can label the issue more specifically. The question form is respectful and also allows the manager to say if the time or place is not suitable for the conversation.

A useful general question is: Can we talk about something that is concerning me? Alternatively, you could be a little more specific by asking: Can we talk about something that is getting in the way of our working together?

Then describe exactly what is causing your frustration. Be very specific. It helps if you refer to a recent incident that the manager may also recognize.

The next step is to describe how you feel about the situation. Remember, this is your interpretation and your manager may see it quite differently. You could say: Maybe I am being too sensitive, but I am beginning to feel you do not want any input from me.

Finally, ask for feedback: I am wondering if there is anything I can do to share my ideas with you more effectively. This is a safe way to minimize defensiveness and encourage dialogue.

If you use these steps, you will help your manager understand how their behavior is affecting you. You have not been accusing or giving any reason to become defensive, so it is unlikely that the conversation will result in argument. In the event that they were unaware of their behavior, it may be appreciated that you spoke up, and will be more sensitive in future.

Remember that the best way to make sure someone continues with a behavior is to give him or her positive feedback. If your manager changes their behavior even a little, for the better, be sure to acknowledge it. Everyone enjoys positive feedback!

When you approach difficult conversations using this process, you will open the door to healthy dialogue and better working relationships.

Chapter 11: Military Training

There are four distinct attributes that champion athletes possess. These qualities put them 'over the edge' in their respective sport and can be carried over into other combat sports, business and daily life. Granted, many great athletes possess natural talent, which is a gift, but everyone possesses the ability to gain the skills required to contend at high levels of competition. One significant skill is mental toughness.

Talent along with physical abilities only take you so far simply because they're physical characteristics, which in turn only comprise about 60% of your true potential ability. People must account for the other half of themselves, which happens to be the mental game. The next four attributes undoubtedly are a prerequisite if you wish to be a success.

Be Flexible: Which means that you need to be able to "role with the punches" before, throughout and after competition. Remaining able to change gears in your mind and remain poised, positive, and focused. To be versatile is developing the ability to bend with the instances, which might be out of one's influence. Some matters such as an injury, illness, awful officiating, blown game plans, or whatever negative circumstance imaginable can and do happen. Deciding to move forward into the path that will assist your wants, as opposed to focusing on the dilemma itself is an excellent indicator of a mentally tough athlete.

Be Responsive: This is the ability to remain charged, focused, intense and highly connected in moments of extreme pressure. As the battle heads to the next level, responsive athletes step up their game as the game itself, steps up. These types of athletes are created "clutch" players, or "the go to guys". They do not pull out from the challenge and become unresponsive. This is another indicator of a mentally tough athlete.

Be Strong: Mentally and emotionally strong athletes support the capability to impose as well as resist tremendous emotional force while under significant challenges. In turn this helps them maintain their particular "fighter" attitude. They are not swayed simply by "momentum swings" or "bad calls" or mistakes. They retain the aggression right from the start to the end, regardless of pain, exhaustion, or even the scoreboard. They keep battling since it's putting up the good fight that is crucial to them.

Be Sturdy: Resilient athletes are able to absorb incidents as well as mistakes and recover rapidly while at the same time getting stronger. They put the bad situations behind them and refocus on the particular endeavor-taking place. They recognize that focusing on the situation simply creates many more issues. Thus, being a 'remedy-focused' athlete gives them a lot more choice and allows them to be always pushing forward.

These characteristics need to be consciously changed to habits in order to succeed. You don't need to be considered a superstar to turn into a superstar. Just like the physical aspect of sports, one gets better with "perfect" training, thus does the mental factor. One method to create these four characteristics would be to recite them repeatedly, as well as knowingly trying to catch yourself when you aren't acting within the limitations. By consciously training yourself within these four attributes, they'll at some point develop into habitual actions, and push you towards greatness.

CHAPTER 12: CASE STUDY

This period of the year, I get calls from many golfers who want to qualify for the US Open. Many of the golfers who reach out to me are club pros, teaching pros, college coaches and assistant professionals. For the most part, they are talented players, but only a few have the physical and the mental skills to succeed at this level. Remember, one bad shot or one bad hole can sometimes kill a great round.

Qualifying for the US Open is made more difficult because many of the rounds are played on some tough courses. I have seen many fine players humbled by these difficult venues.

The golfers who come to see me for help are all looking for more confidence, focus and for some kind of mental edge for this big event.

To help golfers prepare for this kind of challenge, I like to watch them play around on a tough course. I tell them that they need to shoot a sixty-nine for the day. This is a respectable score and this number places some pressure on them.

This helps me to see how they handle this kind of challenge. It makes no sense to watch golfers at this level play a leisurely round. They will not learn anything and nor will I learn anything about their game without some pressure on them.

Several weeks ago, I watched one of my clients, Pedro Benenati, a golf pro who teaches at Drive 495 in New York, play the course at Ridgewood Country Club in Ridgewood, New Jersey.

I have known Pedro for about eight months. He is a talented player and a wonderful person. He is not as lengthy a hitter as several players I have trained, but he has a very worthy short game and he knows golf very well. In fact, I am trying to help him to attract some additional sponsors as his mental toughness improves.

I watched Pedro carefully. He wound up shooting a 75 on aerated greens. This was not bad, but he needs to make a few adjustments to reach that magic number of 69.

After the round, we spoke in great detail about how he can improve mentally. To remind him of the key points, I e-mailed Pedro ten tips after the round in New Jersey.

These guidelines had to do with his confidence, his self-talk, his breathing, and his level of aggressiveness, risk taking, pre-shot routine, goal setting and his focus on his putting.

There is very little that he needs to learn about the mechanics of the game. At his level, at this point, in his career, winning is about what is going on between his ears.

Pedro, who is from a family of golf pros, is very cooperative and compliant and he told me he is now integrating these techniques into his game when we spoke this week. He is feeling comfortable and playing well.

Another key issue is peaking at the right time. You do not want to over train or to under train prior to a major event. This is a delicate balance and the right level of training is different for each professional. Occasionally, it can be hard to find the right training time, energy and regime.

The qualifying events are a few weeks away, so Pedro and I are hopeful that he will achieve his goals and his dreams in 2017.

CONCLUSION:

After perusing the above chapters you now know that mental toughness plays a key role in the sustained success of any individual. Be it in the areas of health, sport, business or just life in general. You also know that the particular skill set for mental toughness can be learned with training over time. The proactive measures detailed in this book should be adopted as soon as possible if you think you need to develop any of these areas within yourself, and most of us do. The goal of this material has been to give you the necessary foundations to build upon your mental prowess. Developing your mental toughness will allow you to become more confident and self aware, which will in turn allow you to operate with higher efficiency and effectiveness in relation to achieving the goals you have set. Another thing this book aims to teach is effective goal setting, which myself and many others think is of paramount importance. Before using correct goal setting it felt like I was flying blind, working towards something unattainable, shimmering in the distance. More often than not I would give up on my idea or just let it fade out because I didn't have the correct plan in place. It is my firm belief that in covering the various topics above you will have defined the areas in which to target and develop within yourself. If you choose to do this without hesitation or procrastination you're setting yourself up to live the life of your dreams. A life full of accomplishment, wealth (however you want to define it) and well managed relationships.

Please click link to leave review :)

Click here to check out the rest of Mental Toughness on Amazon.